FREEDOM FORCES

★ HOMELAND SECURITY: ★

A NATION PROTECTED

Carla Mooney

Educational Media
rourkeeducationalmedia.com

Scan for Related Titles and
Teacher Resources

www.rourkeeducationalmedia.com

PHOTO CREDITS: Cover photo by James Tourtellotte, CBP photography, Barbed wire background LanaN; back cover and title page: flag © SFerdon; Page 4 © seal courtesy U.S government, airport photo James Steidl; Page 4/5 © Ints Vikmanis; Page 6 © charles taylor; Page 8 © Dan Howell; Page 8/9 © TSGT CEDRIC H. RUDISILL, USAF; Page 10/11 © James Tourtellotte CBP; Page 11 © Secret Service Seal courtesy U.S government, photo Department of Defense; Page 12 © James Tourtellotte CBP; Page 13 © FBI photo; Page 14 © Billy Hathorn, helicopter photo James Tourtellotte CBP; Page 15 © port photo Charles Csavossy, CBP photography; Page 16 © James Tourtellotte CBP; Page 18 © Boarder Patrol patch courtesy U.S. government, map Hibrida; Page 19 © Gerald L. Nino, dog photo James Tourtellotte CBP; Page 20 © Gerald L. Nino; Page 21 © finger print sheet David Alary, James Tourtellotte CBP; Page 22/23 © Jocelyn Augustino FEMA; Page 23 © FEMA; Page 24/25 © Leonard Zhukovsky; Page 25 © Leonard Zhukovsky; Page 26 © Brian Guest; Page 28 © George Bush courtesy of U.S. federal government, seal courtesy of U.S. government, Hurricane Katrina photo NASA; Page 29 © Deepwater Horizon photo U.S. Coastguard, Hurricane Sandy photo NOAA

Edited by Precious McKenzie

Designed and Produced by Blue Door Publishing, FL

Library of Congress Cataloging-in-Publication Data

Homeland Security: A Nation Protected / Carla Mooney
  p. cm. -- (Freedom Forces)
  ISBN 978-1-62169-926-2 (hard cover) (alk. paper)
  ISBN 978-1-62169-821-0 (soft cover)
  ISBN 978-1-62717-030-7 (e-book)
Library of Congress Control Number: 2013938878

Also Available as:
ROURKE'S
e-**Books**

Rourke Educational Media
Printed in the United States of America,
North Mankato, Minnesota

Rourke
Educational Media

rourkeeducationalmedia.com

customerservice@rourkeeducationalmedia.com
PO Box 643328 Vero Beach, Florida 32964

TABLE OF CONTENTS

CHAPTER ONE SECURING THE NATION

Have you ever wondered why you take off your shoes and scan your bags every time you get on an airplane? Airport security uses high-tech equipment to make sure no one is carrying weapons or explosives. These procedures were created by the Department of Homeland Security (DHS). It is one way the department keeps America safe.

The Aviation and Transportation Security Act in 2002 requires that all passenger screening be conducted by federal employees. As a result, screening is now provided by the Department of Homeland Security.

The Explosive Detection System machines can quickly capture an image of a single bag and determine if a bag contains a potential threat item.

The DHS's mission is to protect the United States from the many threats it faces every day. The Department has five main responsibilities. One of its top priorities is to prevent **terrorism** in the United States and against Americans worldwide. The DHS also secures the country's borders. It ensures that people entering, living, and working in America have legal status to do so. In addition, the DHS protects the country's computer information systems. The DHS is also responsible for helping during disasters such as hurricanes, floods, and tornadoes.

A U.S. passport is required for all foreign travel by U.S. citizens. Your passport serves as a key that allows you to exit and enter the United States.

Keeping America safe is an enormous job. Twenty-two different federal departments and agencies make up the DHS. Each department is an important piece of DHS's ultimate goal, keeping America safe.

U.S. DEPARTMENT OF HOMELAND SECURITY

SECRETARY / DEPUTY SECRETARY

CHIEF OF STAFF

EXECUTIVE SECRETARIAT

MILITARY ADVISOR

MANAGEMENT DIRECTORATE

CHIEF FINANCIAL OFFICER

SCIENCE & TECHNOLOGY DIRECTORATE

NATIONAL PROTECTION & PROGRAMS DIRECTORATE

POLICY

GENERAL COUNSEL

LEGISLATIVE AFFAIRS

PUBLIC AFFAIRS

INSPECTOR GENERAL

HEALTH AFFAIRS

INTERGOVERNMENTAL AFFAIRS

INTELLIGENCE & ANALYSIS

OPERATIONS COORDINATION & PLANNING

CITIZENSHIP & IMMIGRATION SERVICES OMBUDSMAN

CHIEF PRIVACY OFFICER

CIVIL RIGHTS & CIVIL LIBERTIES

DOMESTIC NUCLEAR DETECTION OFFICE

FEDERAL LAW ENFORCEMENT TRAINING CENTER

U.S. CUSTOMS AND BORDER PROTECTION

U.S CITIZENSHIP & IMMIGRATION SERVICES

U.S. COAST GUARD

FEDERAL EMERGENCY MANAGEMENT AGENCY

U.S IMMIGRATION AND CUSTOMS ENFORCEMENT

U.S. SECRET SERVICE

TRANSPORTATION SECURITY ADMINISTRATION

With more than 200,000 employees, the DHS is the third largest Cabinet department, after the Departments of Defense and Veterans Affairs.

CHAPTER TWO

ATTACK ON AMERICA

On September 11, 2001, terrorists **hijacked** four airplanes. They flew the planes into the World Trade Center in New York City and the Pentagon in Washington, D.C. Nearly 3,000 people died in the attacks. Many people had believed that terrorist attacks only happened in other countries. Now, everyone knew terrorists could strike at home.

Along with the 110-floor Twin Towers, numerous other buildings at the World Trade Center site were destroyed or badly damaged.

The Pentagon was severely damaged by the impact of American Airlines Flight 77 and ensuing fires, causing one section of the building to collapse.

After the 9/11 attacks, Congress created the Department of Homeland Security. Its purpose was to improve America's defenses against terrorism. The DHS is the third-largest department in the U.S. government. Every day, DHS employees work to keep America safe from all types of threats, such as terrorism, **cyber attacks**, and natural disasters.

FREEDOM FACT
Every day, the DHS patrols 3.4 million square miles (8.8 million square kilometers) of U.S. waterways.

SECRET SERVICE

The Secret Service is an important DHS agency. Secret Service agents protect the president, the president's family, and other important government officials. Secret Service agents also manage security when a foreign official visits.

CHAPTER THREE FIGHTING TERRORISM

One of the DHS's most important goals is to protect America from terrorists. Terrorists can attack in many ways. They may strike with nuclear weapons or explosives. They may release chemical or biological weapons. They may launch cyber attacks.

This CBP or DHS officer uses a high tech device to peek inside a gas tank for contraband.

Under a directive issued by President Bush, and overseen by Office of Homeland Security officials, CIA and FBI officials have created a comprehensive database that could be used by various federal and, in some cases, state agencies.

The DHS works to stop attacks before they can harm Americans. The Department works with the Federal Bureau of Investigation (FBI) and the Central Intelligence Agency (CIA). They collect and share data on possible terrorist activity. The DHS monitors phone calls and e-mails of terror suspects. They use **informants** and spies to learn about possible terrorist plots.

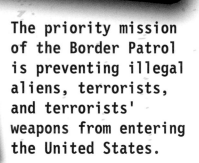

The priority mission of the Border Patrol is preventing illegal aliens, terrorists, and terrorists' weapons from entering the United States.

Within the DHS, the Transportation Security Administration (TSA) is responsible for security at airports and railway stations. TSA workers patrol airports and train stations for suspicious activity. The TSA also scans passengers and baggage for weapons and explosives. They travel on flights to prevent plane hijackings.

The U.S. Coast Guard patrols the waters around the country to prevent attack by sea. U.S. Customs and Border Protection screens people crossing the border to make sure terrorists do not sneak into the United States from another country.

The Border Patrol operates ATVs, motorcycles, snowmobiles, and boats near rivers.

The DHS also protects the country against nuclear, chemical, and biological attacks. Radiation detection technologies scan all cargo and personal vehicles entering the country. **First responders** use handheld scanners that can detect chemical weapons. Sensitive systems can detect the release of biological weapons. In addition, scientists are working on new devices to detect even the tiniest amounts of these deadly weapons and prevent attacks.

Customs and Border Protection has the capability to check and evaluate hazardous materials.

THE NATIONAL TERRORISM ADVISORY SYSTEM

In 2011, the DHS introduced a system to warn Americans about threats. Threats are put into either **elevated** or imminent categories. The DHS makes public announcements when it has new information about threats.

CHAPTER FOUR SECURING BORDERS

America shares 7,000 miles (11,265.41 kilometers) of land on the border with Canada and Mexico. There are also many rivers, lakes, and coastal waters that surround the country. Protecting these borders is an important part of keeping America safe.

U.S. CUSTOMS AND BORDER PROTECTION
U.S. DEPARTMENT OF HOMELAND SECURITY

CANADA

UNITED STATES

MEXICO

Several DHS agencies guard America's borders. U.S. Customs and Border Protection (CBP) and the U.S. Coast Guard patrol land and sea borders. U.S. Immigration and Customs Enforcement (ICE) investigates goods and people entering the United States illegally. Together, these agencies prevent terrorists and weapons from entering the country.

CBP Border Patrol Marine units patrol the waterways of our nation's borders.

Canine agents help keep our mail, borders, planes, ships, and cities safe from illegal drugs, explosives, and other dangerous items.

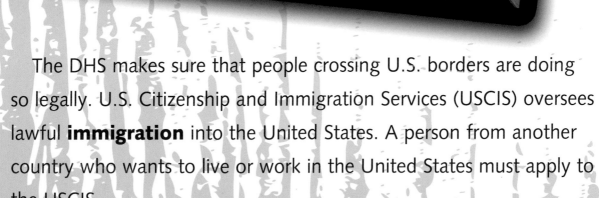

The DHS makes sure that people crossing U.S. borders are doing so legally. U.S. Citizenship and Immigration Services (USCIS) oversees lawful **immigration** into the United States. A person from another country who wants to live or work in the United States must apply to the USCIS.

BIOMETRIC IDENTIFICATION

Biometrics are unique physical characteristics like fingerprints that identify people. Biometrics are reliable and almost impossible to forge. The DHS checks a person's biometrics against a list of known or suspected terrorists and criminals. This helps the DHS stop suspected terrorists before they enter the United States.

A Border Patrol agent uses an automated fingerprint recognition system to process an individual who entered the U.S. illegally.

CHAPTER FIVE

PREPARING FOR DISASTERS

When a fierce flood, hurricane, tornado, or blizzard strikes, many people can be injured or killed. Millions of dollars of property may be destroyed or damaged. The DHS helps Americans prepare for and recover from a natural disaster. The Federal Emergency Management Agency (FEMA) oversees the government's response to disasters.

Protect Your Pet!

Betty lives in a coastal area and FEMA made sure a pet life jacket was included in her owners' emergency supply kit.

FEMA rescues a flood victim. The agency's primary purpose is to coordinate the response to a disaster that has occurred in the United States and that overwhelms the resources of local and state authorities.

In 2012, Hurricane Sandy devastated the northeast United States. More than one hundred people died. Thousands of homes flooded. Millions of people lost electrical power. The DHS and FEMA sent more than 2,200 employees to help with recovery efforts. Federal urban rescue teams helped save more than 700 people. Others set up large electrical generators to power hospitals and nursing homes. Still others cleared roads of debris. FEMA also opened disaster recovery centers to help people affected by the storm.

FREEDOM FACT

The DHS trains thousands of first responders nationwide about what to do in a disaster or emergency.

Aftermath of Hurricane Sandy, 2012.

CHAPTER SIX
PROTECTING AGAINST CYBER ATTACKS

Americans rely on computer systems every day. Power grids, energy systems, banks, hospitals, and other important services use computer systems to operate. A large cyber attack on these systems could shut down many key services.

DHS computer engineers, scientists, and analysts work together to prevent cyber attacks. **Surveillance** systems monitor the government's computers for suspicious activity and potential attacks. The Department works with Internet service providers, businesses, and others around the country. It also issues alerts to warn the public about threats. Homeland security is a tremendous operation that works diligently to keep Americans safe.

An attack on the U.S. power grid could cause billions of dollars in damage and thousands of deaths.

CAREERS WITH THE DHS

It takes many people working together to keep America safe. Homeland Security employees patrol borders, airports, seaports, and waters. They research and develop state-of-the-art security technology. They are the first responders to natural disasters, terrorist attacks, or other emergencies.

To learn more look up
http://www.dhs.gov/careers

TIMELINE

2001:
Terrorists attack
World Trade center
and Pentagon.

2003:
Congress establishes
the Department of
Homeland Security.

2002:
President George
W. Bush signs the
Homeland Security
Act into law.

2005:
Hurricane Katrina
hits the Gulf Coast.

2010:
The Deepwater Horizon oil rig explodes. The DHS helps the Gulf Coast recover.

2012:
Hurricane Sandy devastates the Northeast.

2011:
The DHS introduces the National Terrorism Advisory System.

2013:
Boston Marathon bombing; Homeland Security and Emergency Management training and grants help the city deal with the bombing.

HOMELAND SECURITY
ADVISORY SYSTEM

SEVERE
SEVERE RISK OF
TERRORIST ATTACKS

HIGH
HIGH RISK OF
TERRORIST ATTACKS

ELEVATED
SIGNIFICANT RISK OF
TERRORIST ATTACKS

GUARDED
GENERAL RISK OF
TERRORIST ATTACKS

LOW
LOW RISK OF
TERRORIST ATTACKS

SHOW WHAT
YOU KNOW

1. Why was the Department of Homeland Security founded?

2. What are the five basic responsibilities of the Department of Homeland Security?

3. How many departments and agencies are in the DHS?

4. What DHS agency responds during a natural disaster?

5. How could a cyber attack affect Americans?

GLOSSARY

cyber attacks (SY-bur uh-TAKZ): attacks on computer and information systems

elevated (EL-uh-vay-tid): increased

first responders (FURST ruh-SPON-durz): emergency medical workers who are the first people to arrive at a disaster or emergency

hijacked (HYE-jakd): took illegal control of a plane or other vehicle

immigration (im-i-GREY-shun): coming from one country to live permanently in another country

informants (in-FAWR-muhnts): people who give information, often to law enforcement

surveillance (sur-VAY-luntz): a close watch kept over a person or thing

terrorism (TARE-ur-iz-uhm): the use of violence and threats to spread fear and make political statements

Index

Websites to Visit

http://www.dhs.gov/

http://www.whitehouse.gov/issues/homeland-security

http://www.dhs.gov/national-terrorism-advisory-system

About the Author

Carla Mooney has written many books for children and young adults. She lives in Pennsylvania with her husband and three children. She enjoys learning about U.S. history and reading stories of everyday heroes defending America.

Meet The Author!
www.rem4students.com